CPSIA information can be obtained
at www.ICGtesting.com
Printed in the USA
FSHW022252311021
85871FS

9 781655 851551